ALICIA KEYS songs in A minor

"How Come You Don't Call Me" omitted due to licensing restrictions.

ISBN 0-634-03776-5

HAL•LEONARD®
CORPORATION

7777 W. BLUEMOUND RD. P.O. BOX 13819 MILWAUKEE, WI 53213

Visit Hal Leonard Online at
www.halleonard.com

PIANO & I

Words and Music by
ALICIA KEYS

GIRLFRIEND

Words and Music by ALICIA KEYS,
JERMAINE DUPRI, JOSHUA THOMPSON,
ROBERT DIGGS and RAYMOND JONES

Original key: G♭ major. This edition has been transposed up one half-step to be more playable.

* Vocals written one octave higher than sung.

FALLIN'

Words and Music by
ALICIA KEYS

TROUBLES

Words and Music by ALICIA KEYS
and KERRY BROTHERS

Original key: A♭ minor. This arrangement has been transposed down one half-step to be more playable.

me, ba - by,) _____ all you do is let me know. ___ Why ___

___ does ___ it feel that ___ my mind_ is con - stant - ly ___ try - ing ___

8vb throughout

___ to pull __ me down? __ I ____ can't _ seem __ to __ get __ a - way. ___

ROCK WIT U

Words and Music by ALICIA KEYS,
TANEISHA SMITH and KERRY BROTHERS

There's no es - cape __ from __ the spell ___ you __ have placed __

deep in my heart and my mind. Fool - ish am I ___ your

pow - ers __ to try, ___ to ev - er leave __ you be - hind. __

Vocals written one octave above recorded pitch.

Dead broke;_ no job,_ no house,_ no ride,_

I'm gon - na stay_ right by_ your side._

I wan - na rock wit you,_

Lead vocal ad lib: (Come give me

all your love.)_

no mat - ter what we do,_

(I wan - na

with you and on - ly you.

I wan - na rock wit you.

I wan - na rock wit you,

no mat - ter what we do,

with you and on - ly you.

I wan - na rock wit you.

I wan - na rock wit you,

no mat - ter what we do,

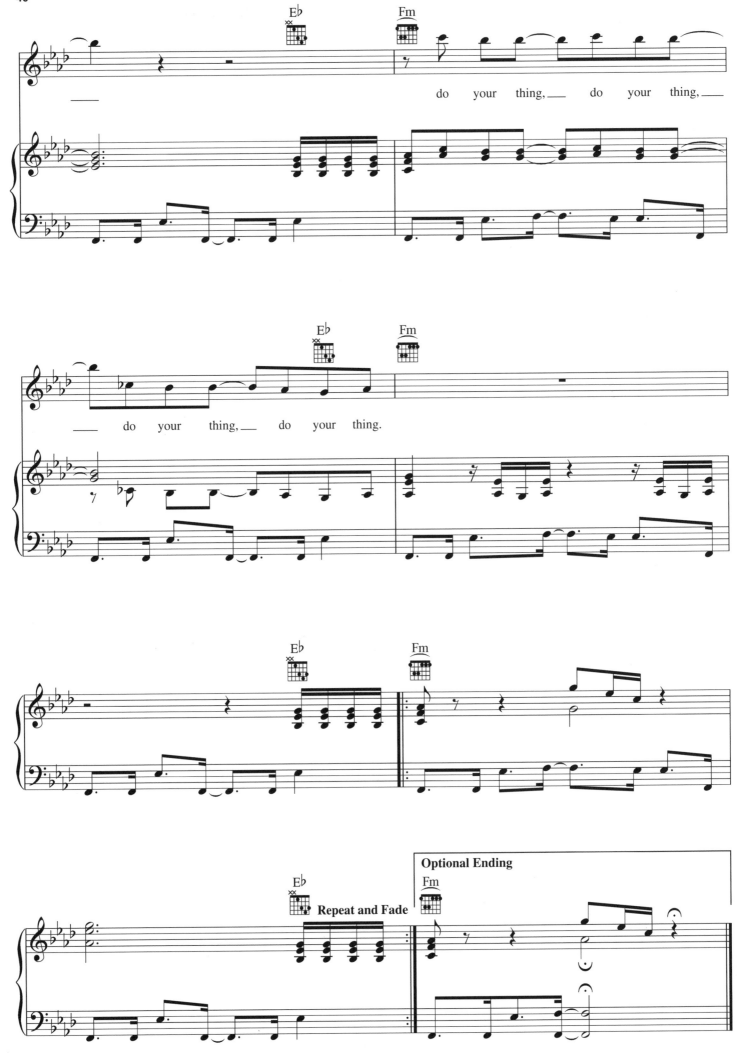

A WOMAN'S WORTH

Words and Music by ALICIA KEYS
and ERIKA ROSE

JANE DOE

Words and Music by ALICIA KEYS
and KANDI L. BURRUSS

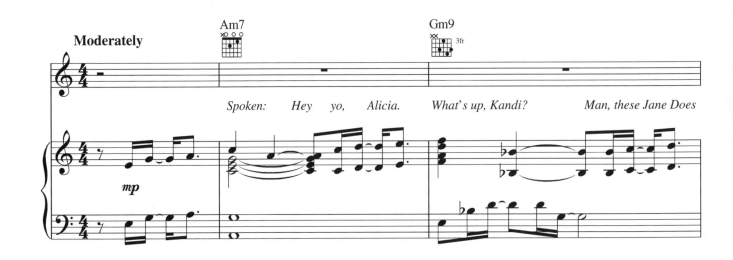

Spoken: Hey yo, Alicia. What's up, Kandi? Man, these Jane Does

be killin' me, thinkin' they're slick with it. For real. Drop the beat. Alicia Keys.

Kandi. Collabo.

GOODBYE

Words and Music by
ALICIA KEYS

Moderately, in 2

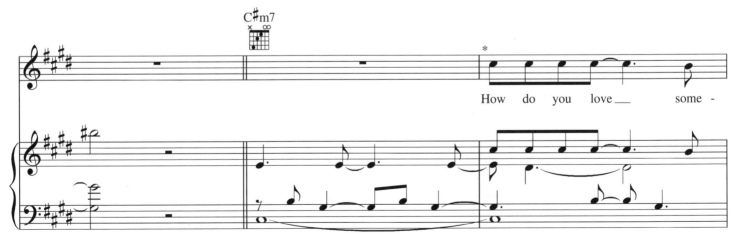

*Vocals written one octave above recorded pitch.

THE LIFE

Words and Music by ALICIA KEYS,
TANEISHA SMITH and KERRY BROTHERS

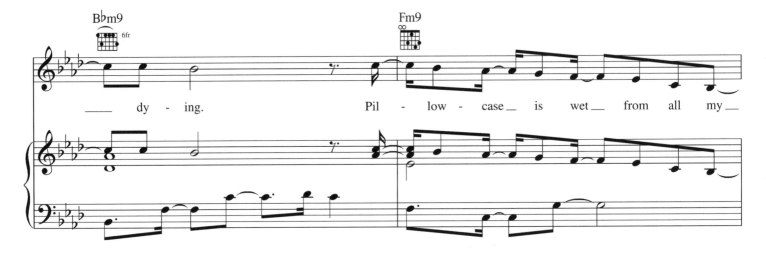

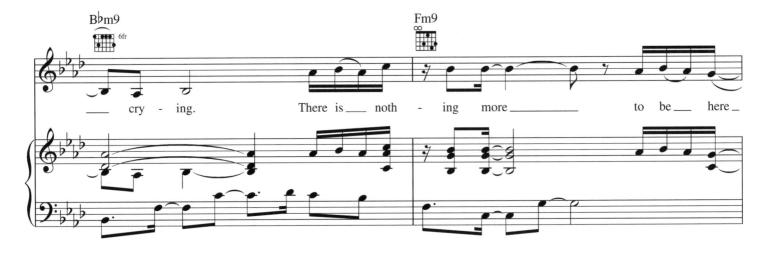

(This   is   the   life.)

(Y - yeah, y - yeah, _ y - yeah, y - yeah, y - yeah, y - yeah.) _____

MR. MAN

Words and Music by ALICIA KEYS
and JIMMY COZIER

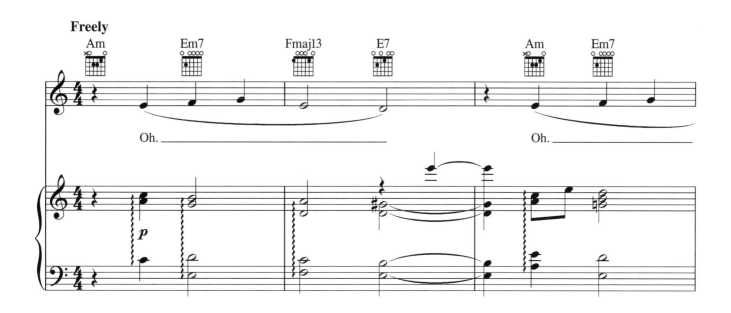

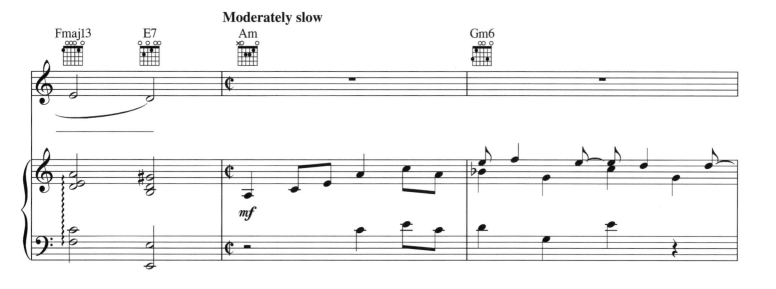

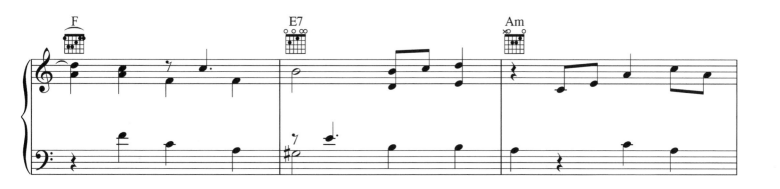

*Both times: sounds one octave lower than written.

NEVER FELT THIS WAY

Words and Music by BRIAN McKNIGHT
and BRANDON BARNES

BUTTERFLYZ

Words and Music by
ALICIA KEYS

WHY DO I FEEL SO SAD

Words and Music by ALICIA KEYS
and WARRYN CAMPBELL

*Vocals written one octave higher than recorded.

Oh, _____ I just want it to be _____ how _ it

used to be, _____ yeah, ___ 'cause I wish that I could stay. ___

But in time, ___ things must _____ change. _

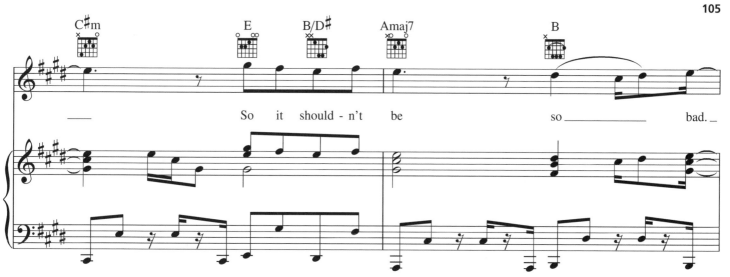

So it should-n't be so _____ bad. _

So __ why do I feel _____ so sad? __

By now _____ (Lead vocal ad lib.)
(Repeats ad lib.)

CAGED BIRD

Words and Music by
ALICIA KEYS

*Vocals written one octave higher than recorded.

fly, fly, fly, _____ the whole world _____ to _____ see. _____

She's _____ like _____

a caged _____ bird.

Fly, _____ fly. _____

_____ Ooh, _ just let her fly, _ just let her fly, just let her

fly, _____ spread _____ her wings, spread beau -

- ty, mm.

LOVIN U

Words and Music by
ALICIA KEYS

Spoken: Yeah, let me, let me try something real quick.

Sung: If I gave you for-ev-er, _____

would you take care of me, yeah ___ yeah (ah - ooh)? Would you take me for

Original key: B major. This edition has been transposed up one half-step to be more playable.